People Suck

By

Jeff M<u>c</u>Carley

jeff.mccarley.author@gmail.com
A WRITTEN BY VETERANS publication

For Mom & Dad

Table of contents

People Suck

How to become a legend 101

The flight line of an air station is a very busy place. And by flight line, I mainly mean a strip of thoroughfare between the hangers and the aircraft staging area. There entails parallel and perpendicular comings and goings by everything from dumbass Marines stomping worn heels into the non-skid; any manner of Ground Support Equipment (GSE), big and small; white Government Owned Vehicles in all sorts of goofy-looking varieties; and even entire aircraft (birds) that are being pushed or pulled by more GSE into or out of an ancient hanger. All of this congestion, which we refer to as a gaggle-fuck, is quite dangerous at times. So not only do Marines have to look out for other Marines, but we also have to look out for the Commandant's equipment, too, of course.

My flight line was the gem of the Corps - Marine Corps Air Station Yuma, Arizona. Well, to be specific, I was fifty-one Alpha (51A), Airframes, Marine Aviation Logistics Squadron 13, Marine Aircraft Group 13, 3rd Marine Air Wing. The trick is to use Marine as many times as possible to insure that people know you're talking about Marines. It really does roll off of the tongue, though. Try it – fifty-one Alpha, Airframes, MALS-13, MAG-13, 3rd MAW, with 51A being my work center.

I was a sheet metal smith and performed advanced composite material repairs and fabrication. I know, who gives a shit, right? All that matters is that I was a part of the second level up in maintenance. Marines at the O-level (squadron) were always breaking shit, so they sent it to us at the I-level, then we would perform severely under budgeted magic for Uncle Sam. Since the pilots were also Marines, and the birds were also Marines, they were always breaking shit and sending it up to us.

The stretch of flight line outside of the Airframes building wasn't too busy most of the time because the four AV-8B Harrier squadrons were at the other end - VMA-214 Blacksheep, VMA-311 Tomcats, VMA 513 Flying Nightmares, and VMA 211 Avengers. In order to make up for an inordinately quiet and peaceful strip of flight line, The Corps' nearly flawless wisdom would do things like temporarily assign a training squadron of Hueys to the visitor's hanger next to Airframes, but park the entire squadron near the Airframes building and mobile deployment vans. Not in front of their own hanger, two hundred yards from us, like the rest of the Marine Corps. If you've never watched a brand new pilot taxi a helicopter with skids (no wheels) into position, then I can really only compare it to a monkey trying to fuck a football.

When high velocity rotors, like those on a helicopter, hit something - say re-enforced concrete, for example, or a parked helicopter - those rotors tend to explode. Marine Corps aircraft always park in formation (a squarish grid). The closest edge of that formation was always about way-too-close-to-me yards from the Airframes hyd shop (hydraulics shop) vans. The vans were really just fancy shipping containers like you see on cargo ships and trains. Staged near the Airframes building, they were designed to be dropped into the middle of nowhere and to be set up quick and easy as maintenance buildings. Very light. I wouldn't trust those flimsy things to stop a bean bag and there were Marines inside pretending to work.

In a cubby between vans, facing the flight line, us Non NCOs and Corporals would smoke. Non NCO is a double negative that denotes nobody-ness in the so labeled, and a Corporal's only true rank is to answer for the fuck-ups of the afore mentioned nobodies. We tended to collect in dark corners to avoid any number of unwanted things. Usually we smoked and sometimes we even smoked just outside the yellow line. The yellow line was the outside edge of the flight line and the red line parallel to it was the official start of the fight line, the thoroughfare of chaos I mentioned earlier. There was no smoking on the flight line, so we made sure not to touch the yellow line. Rules are orders, after all.

So there we would sit, kneel, or stand and tensely watch these horribly new Huey pilots pitch and yaw, tip front to back, and side to side, as they struggled desperately to fly straight in any fashion, and at altitudes as low as the ground. High velocity bomb material whizzed by the pavement, mocking every stander-by smoking instead of working. I've seen a tail rotor come as close as two feet from hitting the ground and becoming an all-night repair for someone. Like I said before: pilots are Marines, too.

Despite such perils, we still finished our cigarettes. Then most of us threw the butts in the general direction of the butt-can, but not into it. That seemed to be Standard Operating Procedure Marine Corps wide.

Also, like I said before, my stretch of flight line was pretty quiet, especially on the night shift.

Us Non NCOs loved night crew because all of the brass and rockers up front were gone during our shift. Not only does that translate to a three-quarter reduction in Marine Corps day-to-day bullshit, but it comes with a low likelihood of being voluntarily told to do some shit-detail.

There was a Staff Sergeant at Airframes, SSGT Richard, who would look at one Marine and bark an order with another Marine's name, then later threaten to write-up a third Marine for not following that very same order. He led from the front, you see, so he wasn't so good at matching up names and faces. He wasn't so good with whether he was in your direct chain of command or not, either. He even came into the shop early one Sunday morning while we finished up a Priority-One repair. SSGT Richard asked us where everyone was and we told him that it was Sunday morning. As he walked off, he still looked confused and unconvinced.

It required cunning and good instincts to navigate through the day shift duty roster without being assigned to unfuck a fucked-up shitter or clean up the smoke pit because the Sergeant Major saw it. And every Marine is a janitor because cleanliness is next to idleness. So yeah, night crew was great. Low supervision.

Most of a structural mechanic's responsibilities were fulfilled in our shop, separate from the aircraft. We broke our gear in private. There were jobs that we had to perform on the bird directly, however. Heavy hardware was a must with any job and we had to lug that gear to the opposite side of the flight line. It was not permitted in POVs, however. We AirWingers didn't lug our heavy gear around like ground pounders and bullet catchers, though. No way. We had GSE. For that purpose, we had the Taylor Dunn. And everyone loved the Taylor Dunn.

That GOVy, our brilliant if not pint-sized piece of GSE, was a white, blocky, miniature truck made from sheet metal, and was propelled by the little gas-powered engine that would. This armored golf cart hit twelve miles-per-hour downhill with the wind on its back and turned corners like a skateboard. But given the time, that thing would get any load up to ten miles per hour. We took no man's word for anything. The Taylor Dunn would scream and growl all the way to the opposite end of the flight line, then it would scream and growl all the way back to MALS-13 Airframes. And sometimes, like any Marine, the Taylor Dunn would leave a visible and fowl smelling odor behind. But I think that he only did that when we drove by all the squadrons, by the Marines that would routinely fuck-up our birds.

One horrible evening, like most others, Lance Corporal (LCPL) Passenger and I were

6

assigned to replace a pylon bearing, which has to be done directly on the wing. LCPL Passenger was a great friend and was at least present at the occurrence of a number of my stories. But in this case, it was me and him because he was a Certified Deficiency Inspector and I was present and accounted for. We loaded the gear onto the Taylor Dunn's flat bed, secured only by wood gates on each side to bounce off of, and we putted off, me at the helm. Taylor Dunn was not the most comfortable ride, as he was small. The front end was just a sheet of steel and it loomed inches from the knees; the seat was straight up and down, and it vibrated like a Harrier. Oh, and of course, driver and passenger practically sat in each other's laps. The job went smoothly, I suppose, because I don't even remember which squadron it was for and I'm actually assuming that it was a bearing.

Upon returning, I zoomed along the yellow smoke line and by the nearly empty butt-can, then executed a starboard (right) turn onto the throughway that ran between the hyd shop vans and the Airframes building. With the MALS-13 GSE maintenance building directly ahead, I headed for the Taylor Dunn's parking spot inside of an alcove in the cinderblock building that enclosed 51A. The opening was about ten or twelve Taylor Dunns wide with doors everywhere.

The hazmat locker to the left, the big double doors and crane ahead and left, the normal door next to that, two soda machines in the right corner, then, on the right wall, parallel to the parking spot, the door that lead directly into the 51A locker room.

Although there was plenty of space in this alcove, I was always worried that I was gonna be run down by the Taylor Dunn when I stepped through the door from the locker room. We parked it five feet from the door, in front of the vending machines.

I turned in so that I was mostly straightened out by the time I went under cover of the alcove. As I was coasting into position and I depressed the brake to ease to a stop, but my foot slipped off of the right edge of the highly polished brake pedal, and the right edge of that same boot sole floored the gas briefly before the pedal popped back up, trapping my foot between the gas and the brake. I tried to pull my foot out to stomp on the brake, but the next thing I remember is looking at a white circle in the windshield, confused, and LCpl Passenger holding his knee, grimacing in pain.

CPL Answers and LCpl Chillin' ran through the regular door near the big double doors. I've still never seen eyes so wide as they stared at the carnage. The Taylor Dunn absolutely crushed the

8

bottom of the left vending machine's door and sat about halfway inside; it had broken the steel bolts that held the three-quarter inch steel brackets to the concrete, anchoring the machine in place, and it crumpled the metal on the machine's back where it was pushed into the cinderblock window sill.

I suffered a minor cut to my forehead and LCpl Passenger rammed his knee into the front wall of the Taylor Dunn. CPL Answers and LCpl Chillin' were sitting in the office on the opposite side of the wall when I rammed the machine like a Roman battle ship. They reported the impact as sounding like "a bomb went off".

I caught a lot of hell over that, but the only thing I actually did wrong was drive the Taylor Dunn without the proper GSE license for that particular piece of equipment. The rest was just my brand of luck.

The civilian's insurance covered all damages to the vending machine and the Taylor Dunn only needed a new windshield. I heard scuttlebutt later on that made me anything from blind drunk to trying to get out of the Corps. But it was just a stupid accident.

For official disciplinary action, LCpl Passenger and I were written up in our Maintenance Logs for misuse and abuse of GSE equipment, and we were made to lead a training for Airframes on the safe and proper use of GSE equipment. I read aloud – Airframes laughed; LCpl Passenger read - I tried not to laugh. Not hard enough, apparently, because I was issued a standard "You better..." ass chewing by SSGT Richard. But he got my name right, every time.

It was then that I knew that I was a legend, for even SSGT Richard knew exactly who I was. Oorah!

Who are he said am crazy?

     Have you ever met a crazy person? If not, does that make you the crazy person? Once as a kid, I a saw a "crazy" woman while we drove through an intersection in our bronze, Ford Aerostar. At three o'clock in the afternoon and in the summer heat of the San Fernando Valley, this woman wore layers of clothing as though the temperature was sub-zero. Blood poured from her nose and off of her chin, and her red hair was matted and knotted as it flung this way and that. She stood in the middle of the crosswalk yelling at someone, or everyone. Back and forth, him and her, the crazy homeless lady had a problem with everyone, and she had a problem with all of the cars. People walked and drove by her cautiously, and they looked over their shoulders as they walked or moved away from her.

     The reason why this woman was ranting insanely, in the eyes of the passersby, was that her interpretation of the environment differed significantly from that of most around her. But in her eyes, the world around her was hyper dangerous. The thing about crazy, though, is that, not only is it a sudden onset episode, but crazy is also contagious.

One busy evening at Barnes & Noble, with but a single register open, I felt fortunate to happen across the line with only one person in it. A tall man, maybe mid-forties, stood at the head of our fledgling line. With my peripheral vision, I could see him looking over his shoulder at me and biting his fingernail. This man's khaki shorts put the "short" in "shorts", and his polo shirt was made from money. Although I can't estimate the shirt's cost, I am confident the man's shoes set him back more than my entire ensemble's worth. But then again, so did my Vans.

I wore said Vans, worn jeans, a t-shirt, and over that my camouflage uniform blouse with long sleeves, the patches, all of it. To tie the look together, I sported an unintended beard and just enough hair to have bed head. The book I held must have complimented the look well with red-flag words like Bipolar and Mood Disorder printed on the cover,

This guy had no shame. I moved my eyes and caught him looking at the name and service patches, then we made eye contact, to his surprise. He just averted his stare to the table behind me, continuing to bite his nail. He never turned his head to its actual business ahead of him.

I looked at the unnecessary impulse items on the shelves in front of me while this guy just continued to watch me and work on that fingernail. I let it go because I could have had a booger on my forehead or something, so why cause a scene and look a fool?

Finally, his turn came, and he walked away. I waited patiently, then my turn arrived, but he didn't walk away from the one open checker. I paused before approaching the cashier because he stayed near the register station. The cashier reminded me that she could help the next guest, so I walked about a mile to the other side of the cash register banks. For some reason, the store chose not to open one of the registers near the front of the line, but instead near the end of the line.

I made it to the register finally, and this guy was still standing one step back from the counter, and one step from my nerves. So I stopped one step from the desk counter and two steps from this man biting that one nail, and then I set my book down. I acted like his behavior was normal, but I really wanted to stare at him until he became uncomfortable. The girl did her thing, which included questions about club cards and discounts. I told her that my wife had one. She punched the phone number into the computer, found the account, and confirmed my wife's name was the one on the account. Through all of that, she split her attention between her duties and this man who is looking over his shoulder, wearing his teeth down on that nail, and sticking his face into my business. Finally, Sir Douche speaks.

"Do you need to scan this again?" as he held out his kid's book.

I know that voice. I know this man. Who is he?

"No," was the official verdict from the cashier. The entire time I inched back to maintain an arm's length from the nail muncher, and the whole time Sir Douche's kids ran in circles around the front of the store, putting their dirty hands on everything. Sir Douche's only effort at controlling his kids was to prevent them from running behind him, which was one step from me. I had no choice but to move closer to him, however, once the pivotal moment had arrived. The moment in which one must part with one's money and leave.

I paid, said yes please to a bag, and tried to leave. In front of me was this slow-moving, Polo shirt clad Sasquatch, now suddenly trying to wrangle his dozen or two kids. They just kept running around him, by me, toward the exit, on the tables, on the walls, and on my patience. I pulled over to the side a few paces from the door and waited as this man's wife came from elsewhere in the store, light-speed in high heels, with still more kids.

I've seen that woman. Who is she?

In front of me, blocking my way to the rest of the world, was Sasquatch and his pod. His pant-suited wife joined him, along with the rest of the fawn, as he lumbered in my way. This woman's clothing was also hemmed from cash, but her sense of style was offset by the budget brand clothing that their kids' wore. As the Douche Troop drained from the store, and as I started to walk that way myself, a girl in a blue shirt, about nine years old, ran by close enough for me to feel the wind of her wake. She ran after the retreating family.

When I made it to the door, the blue-shirted girl was holding open the inner door and trying to figure out what her mother was frantically whispering to her. Lady Douche held the outer door open from outside of the building. She gestured for the girl to hurry to her.

The girl finally let go of the door and rushed by her mother who urged her out with hand gestures and choppy language. I paused in the middle of the foyer because this woman wore a look of fear on her face as she was frozen in place, holding the door open. I stood for what seemed like a fortnight, but the woman just continued to awkwardly hold the door halfway open. I put my hand on the outer door, as far from her as I could, but she just stood there, staring straight ahead of her.

I never received any of the door's weight. Through the little space that Lady Douche didn't occupy in the narrow opening, I had to sidestep to get through the door without touching her. I stopped in the middle of the storefront walkway because the direction I needed to go was blocked by my fan club. Screw it, I thought to myself, and after waiting for a few cars, I crossed there and cut through the third row of cars instead of using the walkway.

I had to cross several columns of cars en route to the strip where my car was parked. As I approached the back end of a pricey, new family car, Lady Douche met me at the passenger corner with two kids, one hand in each of hers. I stopped abruptly to once more avoid making physical contact with one or more of these people. Again I sidestepped to get by her and said, "Whoops! Excuse me".

I walked quickly to the end of that column and boarded my own vehicle, and that 2001 Honda CRV was wearing his battle scars proudly. I pulled out and had to wait to get onto the main driveway. I looked into my rearview mirror and there behind me, in a classy white SUV were the faces of Sir and Lady Douche, kids bouncing everywhere behind them. Sir Douche was still biting that same nail as he watched his wife's jaw flap around, and that's when it hit me: Sir Douche was the store manager of a retailer I worked for.

I cannot speak to what my former boss and his wife thought was happening around them, but they acted in a way that was drastically different from the behavior of everyone present. Their behavior was so irrational that even their 9-year-old daughter looked over her shoulder at them like they were a crazy, bleeding, redhead screaming in the middle of an intersection.

The Shirtless Heroes

When I was fifteen, I participated in a white water rafting trip with a young men's group. The youth group's leader was a dedicated man, and he set us up with a lot of awesome field trips. This outing was definitely the wildest trip we took, if not the strangest trip that the Bishop conceived. He was in his mid-sixties at the time.

Bishop set us up with a guide to take us down the Killer Kern. It is shown as "Kern River" on maps, but is "Killer Kern" to the families of the six or seven people who die each season. But Bishop had that covered. The guide had been down the river a few times and wasn't Kern-killed, so he knew how to do it. He also knew what considerations to make in preparation for the adventure.

The Killer was hours away, but Bishop's van was equipped with Nintendo, the radio station of our choosing, and five bored and loud teenagers. I don't know how he did it. We stopped at the finish spot and picked up Bishop's grown son. His van stayed at the end of the route so that they could drive to Bishop's van upriver once we all made it safely downriver, ideally.

Guide met us at the launching point. That's inside jargon for a riverbank where you kiss your ass goodbye and trust your life to a couple pounds worth of rubber and a plastic paddle. Guide informed us that once we were in the water, the only way back to any kind of road is to raft down the river to the next point of anything that actually existed - the end where we left Son's van.

"But no worries, we have the lesson first," Guide told us.

First, Guide explained to us that there was a mix-up with the reservation and all they had was a six-man raft, but he assured us that the eight of us would be fine in it, just a little cramped. Then Guide launched into an explanation of the dynamics of paddle direction and raft navigation, but assured us that we need only follow his instructions as he considered navigation. They went something like;

"Port to aft and starboard to head and paddle hard boys."

Instructions that meant approximately: "Paddle in a circle, while the current carries us downstream, then mess the back of your shorts as the next rapid comes." I'm a Marine, so I speak a little sailor.

Then Guide gave us such life-saving tips as: while in the water, keep your feet at the surface because the strong current can stuff your feet into the rocks and push your body into the water, pinning you to the river bottom.

"Sixer seven people die here every year, and they don't find the bodies 'til later because of stuff like that. Sometimes they never find the body.

"Also, if yer going through a rapid in the water, fight yer hardest to stay away from the large, flat rocks jutting out of the water. The strong current will pin yuh to the rock and drown yuh. I've seen rafts stuck to the rocks and they are stuck there until the water recedes in the fall.

"Also watch out for swirls in the water, even in the deep, calm areas. They can suck yer feet down and hold you under water. But don't worry. Just follow my instructions, and we'll get through everything okay. Okay? Alright, let's go."

We launched smoothly and floated out to the center of the river. This region was deep and calm, but the Guide informed us that "there could be a strong undercurrent that will drag yuh down and drown yuh. So always keep yer feet up."

We practiced following his orders in the calm, deep water with, possibly, a dangerous undercurrent. "Spit and splash, now splash and spit. Good, we're ready. Let's paddle forward."

21

The rapid approached slowly, and we paddled hard into it, as directed. Very little white water was visible from our slightly higher vantage point, and I had no trouble hearing Guide. The craft sped up a little, and as soon as we slid off of the first nothing rock, the big guy in front of me was dunked into the water, and I suddenly found myself floating away from the rubber sanctuary. Half of the group shared in this slow-motion disaster.

I desperately brought my feet up, tried to stay away from every rock I saw, but was ultimately scrapped along whatever rock that the Killer wanted me to scrape. I waded through the entire first rapid in the water and came out the back end just fine. We all collected on a strip of shore and had a good laugh.

"Well, hey guys, look at it this way; we got it out of the way early."

Rapid two, "piddle paddle, polly pippidy" as we approached the next obstructed stretch, and this one had a lot of visible white water. I felt nervous, and this one was growing louder and louder. We were engaged in some serious adventuring.

The current grabbed the craft and pulled us into the stormy water. We went over a large, flat rock that was visible but submerged, and the front half of the raft disappeared. As we soared

22

over the rock, the big guy, now behind me, went into the water with his piece of the boat and I was pulled out of the boat by the current. I, along with the only other light-weight person, was in the water again, at the start of the rapid. The rest of the group made it through the torrent of water fine once they ditched us.

That rocky patch didn't have any massive rocks, and I managed to avoid the medium boulders, but I hit, scrapped, or was jabbed by every smaller stone as a passing fee. Pushing was sometimes possible, but not always. I fought hard to keep my feet from being stuffed underneath a rock, and I inhaled a lot of water. Rapid Two was much longer than the first. It was probably a good ten miles long or so.

A new strip of shoreline near the calm appeared, and I swam to it. The successful rafters were waiting for Skinny and me when we washed up. Smiles were shown brightly at us, but no laughs this time.

"Soary guys. I've never gone into that rapid from that opening before. I didn't really know what to expect."

Number three announced its presence early.

"Listen carefully guys, this'un is loud."

We were torn from the calm and Guide spit the orders through the air with saliva.

"High fiddly dee, four from seven makes three."

I don't recall the rapid well because the entire boat was just suddenly in the water and then it shot out ahead of us. I don't know how we retrieved the raft, but it definitely beat us through the rapid. No laughs, no smiles, just sitting around.

"Oh, wow. This's never happened before. Ev'ryone just rest fer now. Yer gonna need yer energy."

I can't recall just how many rapids I waded through because my memories are mostly only short bits of the rough spots and the scary moments. I went into the water at the start of every rapid, and I can tell you that the louder the water is, the worse the rocks are. Everybody went into the water at some point, but I went into the water every time. And at the start of the roar.

Many times I went the wrong way around a boulder, or down the more turbulent strip. I could hear the difference ahead of time, and I would try to make the path that was not as loud, but I had little to say in the matter.

The Killer is just boulders exposed from erosion and rocks carried down from up the river. I was little more than a leaf going through some of the monumental size boulders. Often, there would be no bank until I had gone through all of the follow-up rapids. They were usually smaller, but one of them hit my tail bone good.

One section of river that I remember well went through two giant boulders that looked like the world's largest butt. The crack, which was the only way past the ass, was a horrible rock collection that was like stairs. The buttcrack descended about fifteen feet in all. I bumped, pushed, scrapped, and slid into a broad, deep clearing where a boulder that rose about ten feet above the water line split the water. The water there was calm but moving quickly. Strong undercurrent?

The kid in front of me, the big guy, he went around to the right, but I was carried left. To the left was an overhang that hung over the water a few feet. The water underneath it swirled like a toilet. A toilet that I fit into.

Of course, I got sucked in. I tried to swim away from it, but no, I went in. I was nudged into the rock about two feet under the overhang. I had to push off the stone wall to get out. It was the second time around when I got a good kick and was able to push myself out.

After the fourth or fifth dip into the water, I fought as hard as I could and barely made it to the shoreline in the strong current. I was exhausted, and so was Skinny. The group stopped for a rest, and I was feeling anxious about getting back into that raft. Just then, two larger guided tour rafts pulled up and onto the shore like a couple of amphibious assault vehicles.

These professional rafters had nice gear. In the middle of the much larger craft was a perch that the guide sat on, operating a set of oars. The pilot also had a bar to push his feet into for leverage. Besides the guide in each raft, there was also three tourists who spent their money wisely.

"Hey, guys. What's up, guys? Is everyone okay, dudes?"

"Who sin charge here, man?"

"Oh hey guys, I'm the guide. I like yer rafts."

"Your raft is overloaded, dude."

"Yeah, yore gonna get summon killed, man."

"Hey what's up dudes? Everyone okay, guys?"

"Well, there was a mix up with the reservation, and..."

"That snow excuse, man, you can... not... cannot raft down river overloaded, man."

"Well yuh see, it's like I said. There was a mix up with are reservations."

"That don't matter, dude. You can't just stick a bunch'a guys in a raft, dude. People die like that, guys."

"Every ear six or seven people die ear. In dem waters."

"The last rapid, guys, is called pinball, dudes. I've seen rafts pinned to the rocks all season, guys."

"Some once gonna die in the pinball, man."

Each boat had room for one more person. These awesome guys took on two of us to reduce weight in our boat, and us two waterlogged skinny guys each got one of those spots.

These two guides wore sandals, no shirt, sunglasses, what looked like underwear, and a Kern River Tours hat each. They could probably run their raft down the river without any help from stupid tourists like us. Especially without tourists who didn't pay.

I was nervous on every rapid, but Shirtless directed us and got the barge and its cargo through each rocky mortuary.

"Right back, left front – Paddle Paddle Paddle. Every one front. Paddle Paddle Paddle"

He made sense, and I even had fun on Pinball as the raft slid this way and that.

Doggonit

I grew up under the tutelage of a swearing do-it-yourselfer. This means that I was given regular lessons on throwing vulgar language around while insulting an inanimate object, or the brand, model, manufacturer, and even designer of that part. The entire mechanism even, if necessary. Every Ford that Dad bought was the last Ford he was ever gonna buy due to the ill intention of the engineers. Of course, Ford wasn't the only word that started with 'F' in those rants. With a background like such, curse words were learned through context long before a definition was attached. And definitely, before any ethical issues with the words were raised.

Sometimes other families' homes felt weird, but I never really knew why. Looking back, however, it could have been because some families didn't cuss at all. In my house, we got commentary on the Fuckers all over the TV, whichever room we were in. At dinner we had running dialogue shouted at the news and even at fictional TV shows. Sometimes the yelling served as a running update on the progress of a repair. Over the sound of the television, video games, and a stereo, I could still hear the name and nature of the current snag during the maintenance of one of the McCarley Family vehicles.

The neighbors were also benefactors of patience with Dad and his cars, and Sean with his guitars. My older brother loved to find out how long his amplifier could play at full volume before it quit working. Like cars, electric guitars need some maintenance. Sean performed a regular sonata of a 40-minute improvised guitar solo and "Fuckin' shit – Shit fuck whore" on vocals for backup. Sometimes a string just wouldn't stay in tune long enough for a single guitar solo, but sometimes a string would break. That's where the shoe meets the wall, and the dent meets the teenager.

Dad always fixed things like that immediately, as though it would multiply if he left it for tomorrow. When we came home from the bowling alley late, and Dad saw the dent in the wall, I was scared, too. Sean was on the ropes. Bye-bye guitar, bye-bye friends and freedom, and hello weeds that need to be picked by hand. But while Dad threw phrases like - no more, fuckin' forget about it - at Sean, he patched the dent up

30

with some putty and a putty knife that seemed to come from nowhere. But Dad always seemed to have whatever random things that any repair could need, which was great until you had to find it.

"It's in the middle toolbox of the six tool boxes on the bottom of the cabinet, it's in the third bottom drawer, two-thirds of the way back, on the left next to the crank ratcheting bolt terrorizer, but under the anti-seize with four quarter-inch washers."

Then he hands you his keys. I don't know how many hundreds of keys were on his rings, but they wore out Dad's back and knees. First three keys on the second ring from the primary key ring unlocked the doorknob, deadbolt, and padlock to the garage door. Then there existed a complex set of toolbox, padlock, and other keys. The cabinet was cool because you only needed one more key and it looked different from the rest. The main toolbox was a nightmare. You had to find five keys, six if you needed something in the bottom compartment. But Dad knew exactly what he had and exactly where it was.

When I returned home one day, and my parents were gone, I entered through my front bedroom window because I didn't have keys to the doorknob and the deadbolt on the front door. However, I easily used my fingers to pry and pull open the window and entered my bedroom. Dad had dealt with this security risk a few days before, but I'd forgotten, as teenagers sometimes do. I went to exit my room, where I turned the doorknob and pulled lightly, but the door caught a little. It happened sometimes. I tugged a little harder, and the door snagged as it opened.

A gate hook Dad installed on the outside of my door swung back and forth with the eyelet that had, until recently, been holding the hook to the door jam. This locked the door shut in theory, should anyone enter from my bedroom window. On the doorjamb was a chunk of missing wood.

In no time, Dad had all tools and materials for the repair from his secret stash somewhere. The missing chunk of doorframe was patched up and the damage painted. In that thirty seconds was a very long ass-chewing that was condensed to only cuss words. Curse words used in various contexts and combinations. I knew exactly what my father was telling me.

I only got weed pulling duty for a week. I think Dad went easy because he knew that that was not a very secure security measure. My noodle arm annihilated that little hook's chance at a career.

Even now I'm not allowed to cuss in front of Mom, though. I'm nervous about her reading this, in fact. Dad and his four boys always chose the gutter mouth, but Mom is squeaky clean. That's why we all know how to speak correctly whether we do or not. Mom snapped at us every time she heard phrases like *he gotts to,* or *fuck-off, asshole.*

Nonetheless, I was an old hand at throwing the word 'shit' around by junior high school. Sometimes, I didn't utter a sentence that didn't end with the word shit. It was in our culture. Jared, my younger brother, and I only cussed at one another, exclusively. When Mom was around, we just didn't speak to each other. But when we played POGs the cork was out of the bottle, and even Mom heard those colors.

While my youngest brother Cory was only forming sentences with a few words, he cussed. One day he was slamming his hand on one of his big truck toys and saying *mannit.* Catching that context, Mom listened to him speak it a few more times within a few seconds and told Cory he wasn't allowed to use that word.

"Daddy mannit, me too mannit," was his two cents on that issue.

Long before that, though, I can clearly remember standing in the key-hole of the cul-de-sac that we lived on, and I wanted to shout something at an older kid, but I wasn't sure if I could say *doggonit.* I ran to the sidewalk, up the street to our house in the middle of the cul-de-sac. Into the house, I dashed, and to my Mom, I ran.

"Mom, can I say *doggonit*?"

"Yeah. You can say *doggonit*."

I don't remember what happened next, but Mom has since told me that I ran out of the house and immediately shouted, "Doggonit, you fuckers!"

Grape Stomp

SHOCK! Everything disappears but the threat. Ready to explode with everything within, push forward, the butthole puckers, tense - Ready. Some are ready to run. Some people freeze. Others fight. That is a sudden and genuine fear for one's life. When that response is a false alarm, the moment of intense focus gives way to the heavy and uncomfortable thump of the heart, ringing in the ears, heavy breathing, and, in a false alarm, many become angry at who or whatever caused the reaction. But false alarm or not, the adrenaline and readiness to run, freeze, or fight are real.

Eastbound on the CA-118 freeway, the flow of traffic was sixty-five miles-per-hour and I kept a significant distance between me and the next car in my lane. The flow of traffic tends to slow quickly in L.A. County, and I drove a boat. As I entered a long curve, I had a light-year or two between a metallic pink Subaru and me.

Suddenly I was closing the gap fast, so I got on the brake, but still, the buffer shrank quickly. I pushed the break as hard as I could without locking the wheels and sliding. The Subaru stopped. I had both feet on the brake, pushing the backs of my shoulders into the seat, my butthole puckered too small to see. I heard a *screech* as the tires slid, briefly, before my frontend met the Subaru's backend.

While the rear end of my car was still very light on the wheels, I felt another impact. Then came another smaller bump, and then I just heard a crash. All of that happened fast. Much too quick to think about it, but once it was done, I continued to push as hard as I could on the brake pedal, with both feet and screamed *fuck* for about five seconds. Then my body relaxed. The reaction was delayed and had I died, it would have been with a horrible expression frozen on my face, while wedged as stiff as a board in the driver's space.

Nobody was hurt, and the only damage to my car was the fiberglass grill piece, the radiator, and the fan. It cost me seventy-five bucks at the junkyard and an entire Saturday. Getting home was fun, though. I had to use surface streets because my cooling system was wrapped around the front of the engine. I also had to shut my car off a few times to let it cool.

The other cars in the collision weren't so lucky. The Subaru's back seat was its new rear end; the guy who hit me needed a new front end.

Some people feel those levels of fear over things that most people would consider harmless. These are known as irrational fears. I have heard fear of spiders described that way because I have described it that way once or a hundred times in the past. After all, spiders weigh milligrams and people way hundreds of pounds. How much more blown out of proportion does it get?

I didn't kill spiders in the house unless they were black widows because spiders eat flies, and flies seem to live for years when they are in the house. I kept one spider around because it ate hundreds of ants. I called him George.

Many years after the accident on the 118, I sat on the concrete threshold to my garage, smoking something. To my left and right, within one foot, were five brown widows - a poisonous cousin to the black widow. These spiders vary from light brown to nearly black, they have light brown around the joints of their legs, and their hourglass markings are orange. Overall they are elegantly beautiful like the black widow.

They differ in many ways from the black widow, however, and these differences drive black widows away. Brown widows don't mind pitch dark, but they are not at all bothered by full sun, either, whereas black widows retreat into the dark for the daylight hours. Brown widows make one web, small and messy, and they stay on that web day and night. Black widows make a new web every night, and the webs are much larger, but also messy. Brown widows are not territorial, apparently, because they set up shop right next to each other, within inches. Brown widows are generally considered to be harmless.

So there I sat on a six-inch tall concrete threshold with brown widows all around me on little webs. They don't hang out too far from the ground, so they were mostly out of the way, but everywhere were those small webs with a widow right in the middle, upside down. I had potted plants and planters all over the patio, and the widows made a web in every corner. There must have been fifteen widows in just that two hundred-square-foot area. Whatever, they weigh milligrams, right?

I finished up my business on the stoop, then stood up and put my stuff away. As I walked from under the metal patio covering I felt a web in my hair, on the back of my head. At first, I was just annoyed. Webs are mostly just a pest that can come back hours later, in bed. Then it occurred to me that I was surrounded by widows and I almost felt that SHOCK, but I kept my cool. The web came from up high, and... it's just a spider, after

38

all. So I went into the house and asked my wife, Suzy, if I had a spider on me. With my back turned to her, Suzy didn't see a spider. I was wearing dark clothing, though. However, she then accused me of being paranoid, which I probably was.

About ten minutes later we were sitting at our computers in the spare room, and I felt a sharp, intense burning sensation on the inside of my left calf muscle. Instinctively a swatted at it and lifted my pant leg. I didn't see any spiders. I did see what looked like a wicked mosquito bite, bright red and glowing. I gloated to Suzy's dismay because I am an ass. I wasn't worried much, however, because somebody told me that, although the brown widow's venom is more potent than a black widow's, they secrete so much less of it that the bite only leaves a numb spot. A wives' tale, if you will.

Each night I looked at the bite, and it was bigger, but it didn't itch at all. That started to worry me. Three nights after the bite, the welt looked like a massive pimple the size of a thumb, with a white head on it and everything. The bite impression of a spider's mandibles was clear to see on top of the swelling. In fact, the white head was one of the mandible marks. I was tempted to express it, as I usually would with an infected wound, but I was worried that I could spread the venom. So in my worry, I made a doctor's appointment for it after Suzy made me. Just milligrams, right?

I managed to get an appointment in the next day or two, and by that point, the wound was a purple dome that protruded from my leg enough that pant legs hurt. It was about four inches in diameter, three inches tall, and the talk of all conversation that I walked passed. The doctor looked at it as I explained how I came to host a purple hemisphere on my leg. I described the bite impression and white head before the marks had been stretched into oblivion. Once I had concluded my statement, she pushed on the dome with her finger and explained that there didn't seem to be any fluid in there because it was firm, not squishy. That meant that there was no pus in the abscess.

She was the doctor, so I just picked up the prescription she gave me and went home to pop pills and get better. Five days into the ten-day round of some powerful double antibiotic, the abscess had grown so large that I could not walk right without brushing or kicking it. The purple dome had a diamond-shaped pyramid underneath it, rising from my calf muscle. The entire inside shape of the calf muscle was gone to the swelling.

I was waiting on the antibiotics, so I didn't make an appointment right away. I made the appointment five days in, only after I kicked the dome a few times in one day and the third kick caught it square. There was constant pain from that point forward, and it didn't really vary. It hurt so bad that I couldn't follow a storyline on the television.

April 10, ten days after the bite, I was again at the doctor's office. This time I knew that there was no way they wouldn't drain it. I was in pain, but also I drove myself there, because that's just how I roll, and I could feel the abscess moving with the motion of the car on the way to the office. I did not want that thing to erupt in my car.

Again, I explain the origin of the planet pushing out of my calf. I told the new doctor that there was indeed pus in there. This doctor poked it with his finger, and he said, "Sorry, I know this hurts."

"It does anyway, so..."

"Well, what I want to do is open that up, clear it out, and pack it."

"Okay. Let's do it."

We moved to the operating room, which was a different room with a different kind of bed in it several doors down the hall. I was disappointed because the doctor leaned the bed back so that I wasn't able to see what they were doing. I regret not saying something. The doctor prepped the wound, warned me about the shot, then proceeded to inject a local anesthetic into the taught water balloon under my skin. That hurt. I've had a needle inserted into the ganglion cyst in my right wrist, and they pulled back, moved, then went back in four times. With the same overall procedure, this Doc was sticking that needle into Mount Infection, pulling it out, and then stabbing the wound somewhere else. That hurt much worse than the cyst. I'm good with shots and pain, but I had to lay back, grimace, and hold myself together for that.

I could see when the doctor was cutting a slit by his body language, and I knew that he was draining it when he said with surprise, "Oh look, there is pus in there."

My leg felt better immediately, even after the anesthetic wore off. Every two days I had to go to the nurse's station and have the wound cleaned out and repacked. After cleaning out the injury, they would use a medical ribbon to fill the hole in. This kept the scar from becoming a crater. I got my first look at the wound two days after it was drained and it was a cavernous hole in my calf. It was awesome to look at as I waited for baby spiders to crawl out.

Several treatments after having the cesspool drained, the nurse didn't like the look of the wound, and she called the doc. The first finger poking doctor came in and looked at it. She appeared as though she wanted to poke it, but just took a sample with a swab and sent it off to the lab. I was prescribed a new antibiotic, but I didn't get the message on my phone. I wasn't waiting to hear from them, either.

I was prescribed another antibiotic on Friday afternoon, but I didn't find out until the following Monday when I came in to have my wound cleaned. A new nurse performed the procedure - I never saw the other nurse again. The new nurse lectured me thoroughly and sternly about the importance of getting my prescriptions promptly after having been prescribed them. In fact, I was treated with a bit of hostility from the nurses' station a few times after that.

At home, I looked up Clindamycin and learned that I had contracted an MRSA infection from my doctor's office. I had gone from a pus-filled volcano on my leg to a cave filled with an antibiotic-resistant bacteria. They were rude and abrasive with me because I gave them a SHOCK when they realized what happened. I scared them, and so they were mad at me. I guess seventy-two hours with an untreated MRSA infection is bad.

All of that cleared up, though, as my shit brand of luck does. The entire issue with the wound, from bite to sealed scar, was about three months. I even saw a quick return of my resolve about spiders. In October our kitchen sink backed up like a kinked water hose. The plumber had to go in from the garage side of the wall, from the poisonous spider side of the wall.

There is no counting how many widows of any color were likely in the garage. An egg sac hatched on our property in the spring. I saw the translucent baby spiders coming down from our metal patio covering on their webs - hundreds of them. Some of them landed in my hair and beard, and I freaked out a bit about that. But that was weeks before the hour of the bite.

I opened the rolling garage door for the plumber, and the sunlight flooded the garage. As we stood and spoke, the door settled with the bottom at the height of my forehead. Right there, a foot or less from my face, was a small brown widow. She was medium brown, khaki-colored legs with her orange hourglass looming. The widow clung to the door on a tiny piece of web. I watched that spider for movement for a few seconds, but I thought of the ordinary spider that I killed in the shower days before. I looked around me on the floor, found a dirty rag and picked it up. I stamped that spider with my

44

thumb and twisted it several times afterward. *Hmpff*. Just milligrams. It felt good to kill that thing.

So that was that. I was cured. Maybe spiders would get an extra split second or two before I kill them. With my cure came time to reclaim my plastic watering can. One day in late spring, I looked into the can, and I saw a messy network of webs all over the inside. I flooded that can and left it.

A few days later I dumped out the water and looked inside. The widow was on her web inside, showing her belly. I tried to blast her out with the hose but the webs held strong and she held onto them. I tried once more to flood her out, but she retreated into the hollow handle, which was above the maximum water line. At this point, I was still keeping the wound bandaged full time, so I abandoned the watering can to the spiders. I looked into the can every two weeks or so, and there she would be, a little bit bigger.

But then I killed the October widow in the garage, and I felt empowered. I tromped up to the can that sat in the exact same spot for about four months, and I used one finger to tilt it and peer inside. Still webby inside but there was no spider.

I took hold of the can with both hands, and I angled it so that I could see down the cavity in the handle. I could not see all of the way to the

45

end, but I did not see a spider. I smacked the can then shook it, then I shook the can and smacked it, but no spider ever emerged.

With it being late in the year and I having seen no visual indicators of the spider, I concluded that I could reclaim my watering can. So I filled it. I watered the east plants, front to back, and then I went back to the hose for a refill. With a fresh fill, I watered the north fence line of my property, but the weather was still dry and the potted tangerine tree used most of the can.

I returned to the hose to fill the can yet again, and I wondered if I could get away with just this one last fill. I still had the bonsai trees to water. First thing is first, so I returned to the North West corner of my property to water the Hollywood Juniper tree. I started at the bottom and wet the soil directly, then I raised the can to water the branches. I held the can by the handle with my right hand, and I used my left hand to lift the bottom and tip the can as I raised it.

I lifted the can to shoulder height, and the sleeve of my right arm receded halfway up my forearm. There on the inside of my forearm, on the bottom skull of my tattoo, directly on the skin, crawled a medium brown colored widow with nearly-white legs. This girl was well-fed in that can, and it showed. Slowly and with articulated coordination, those needlepoint legs moved the

46

massive thorax up my arm, looking to get back into the sleeve of my shirt.

I don't know what my left arm did, but it disappeared. I raised my right arm in the air instinctively to pull the sleeve away from the widow as the widow headed for the safety of my shirt. Then some strange, guttural, and involuntary sound emerged from my mouth. It kind of sounded like I was throwing up after being numbed from the dentist, but it also kind of sounded like a low-voiced infant. The sound sprang from me, and I flung my arm the best that I could without bending my elbow, and with the watering can in my hand.

After I flung the spider, I looked, and it was gone. I looked again, and it was still gone. I looked a third time, and it was still gone. I ran from the corner of the yard, fearful that the spider would come back for me. I hurried across the patio, the same patio of widows, but a few steps from the door it occurred to me that the spider could still be in my clothing. Everything became bright, my heart started to pound, my butt cheeks were pulled up into the hole, and I thought about the long sleeve shirt that I was wearing. SHOCK!

I wanted to hit every square inch of my body as hard as I could at the same time, but I thought, *No. Don't do the first thing that comes to mind.* I was vibrating with anxiety as I stood still long enough to think - *Take clothes off. Can't, I'm outside. Go inside. In the bedroom. Oh, fuck! Get this shirt off!*

I nearly ripped the shirt as I tore it off and tossed it aside, then I rushed into the house, into the bedroom, and I stripped down to my underwear. Every mole was a fright, and I wrenched my back a bit twisting around to look everywhere, but I was okay. No spiders and no glowing domes. I put new clothes on, performed a grape stomp on my old clothes, then I put the old clothes in the garage. I wasn't entirely convinced that they were cleared, but I didn't want to put my arms into everything to turn the garments inside out.

Finally, once the adrenalin had cleared from my system and my heart resumed a reasonable tempo; once the ringing in my ears turned into a headache and once my butthole had unclenched and my cheeks came back out, I realized that five milligrams of spider is a whole lot of spider.

Four rules for killing caterpillars

I have begun the self -torturous hobby that is gardening. If a plant grows something that you can eat, I'll try to raise it, even if I don't like the food that was cultivated. I'll find the right way of frying it, and I'll eat whatever the gophers leave. The biggest threat to every garden in my area, however, is the crop-destroying, dream killing, bounty hunting, and ordinary moth. That same annoying light brown or gray thing that flutters around the light, or right in front of your nose and mouth, that winged nuisance will cause a famine that can starve the world to death. I hate moths. They slowly suck the life from the veins of the hosts that they infect.

There are two types of moths to combat, and they consume in two very greedy ways but with two very different assault tactics. The first moth is the same type of moth that I already mentioned, and it will have you spitting, swatting, and then just outright yelling. Those things start as egg yolks, but then they go on to cause great destruction. But when they destroy my hanging shirts, that's just the icing on the cake from a much older moth. The other end of their bodies laid eggs under the leaves and silks of some innocent plants just trying to reproduce through delicious pacts they've made with animals. Symbiosis.

Moth nightmares hatch as little caterpillars that make their way secretively to anything tasty. The first sign of infestation appears as dying or decaying fruit and buds. When you dig into the problematic plant matter to find the cause, these nutrient bloodsuckers look up from the nutrient vein and say Rah! at you. Let's call them Moth Rah. By the time you see Moth Rah, you are too late - the entire plant, crop, and garden are all likely goners. The plants are healthy but barren. This is why gardening is mostly observation, stress, and agony. For a gardener to yield a harvest that is proportional to the amount of time and work invested, a gardener must have paranoia, camouflage, and night vision cameras. Otherwise, caterpillars will defecate their eggs all over the gardener's hard work, right after a dinner of his wardrobe.

The second moth is not stealthy, and it is not picky. I'll call this juggernaut Fat Mouth. I found four Fat Mouths, an inch or two long, on two of my four chili pepper plants. About a week or so later there were two fatter, four inch long Fat Mouths finishing off the rest of the foliage on the third and fourth plants. They even ate some of the jalapenos. I don't know what happened to the other two, but the last two burrowed into the potting soil. I'm still waiting for them to hatch as I write this.

Those two basic categories of consumer also manifest themselves in the human world, ravaging the fruit of society. And damage control from pests is really all that those in the cursed profession of Consumer Service are blessed with facing daily. And, despite popular cultural misconceptions, handling John and Jane Q. Putz is a skill. Especially when dealing with their loud, annoying, dirty, sticky, smelly, and grabby kids. And don't get me wrong, there were some helper spiders in the garden as well. Great people that made my day better often, and even greater people who disliked the kids and scared them off. The good Consumers could do nothing, however, about a Fat Mouth giving me hell because her fifty-cents off coupon didn't work on all thirty bags of gourmet dog treats. Those expensive treats smelled good enough to eat.

It is the Moth Rahs and Fat Mouths that suck the life from the Soulless Associates that you, as a consumer yourself, chase after as they meander, lost, in the Consumer Stores and

Family Entertainment Centers of this land of opportunity. Caterpillars are the people that don't understand that Soulless Associates have absolutely no reason to aggravate or bother a Consumer in any way. Our days are much better when Consumers are happy. But you see, although the symbiotic Consumers can help a bad day, moths are not interested in what's best for the plant, just themselves.

My soul was aborted when I was left in the fire behind the front register at Drug Store's on my first day. Training Associate walked off for some reason, probably one of the Regular Rahs or Dick Mouths walked in, and she just wasn't feeling it that day. Every Soulless Associate has *that one* customer, and every Soulless Associate is always trying to prevent *that one time* from happening again. I learned early on in the retail business to spot a caterpillar quick, sometimes before they realize that I've caught the scent of their eggs.

Rule 1: <u>Shut up and let the Consumer talk.</u> Trust me, this isn't some training slogan. This might seem obvious, but those who are skilled with Consumers know how tricky that rule really is. New Rahs and Fake Mouths come in looking to start a problem for a wide variety of reasons. The better the soulless can spot them, the better the day goes.

A common tactic of a Fake Mouth is to be loud, aggressive, and in your face. This is a blitzkrieg-style assault. Fake Mouths often look to throw you off guard and to elicit an emotional reaction from you. Don't react. Shut up, let the Consumer talk, and you won't blow your top or cry, or something. If a soulless allows one of these pestilent creatures to continue talking, they will talk themselves out. I've had Consumers yell themselves calm. I've had Consumers lean over the counter separating us and try to physically intimidate me when I didn't react. Just turn to stone and watch the Douche Mouth lose confidence.

"Are you gonna help, man, or what?"

"No."

Caterpillars don't like biting into a dead vein, and Fake Mouths don't like simple answers. Simplicity is difficult to manipulate. I always enjoyed the look on a Stumped Mouth's face when they have just been shut down. They look shocked, then confused, then they either demand a manager or they storm off. These types were that store's typical online reviewer.

These tactics do not work on a Bitchy Rah, however. These Consumers are often times just using a soulless as a yelling post. These animals just yell over anything you say. Again, shut up and let the Consumer yell because that is, in fact, a form of talking. At some point, a Bitchy Rah will run out of belittling and demanding complaints to throw at you.

Rule 2: <u>Always pay strict attention to what a Consumer says and does</u>: Again, don't go with the apparent training video spin on this. The people who make those have never fielded a complaint. Once the afore-discussed Bitchy Rah runs out of words to string together, a soulless can point out every hole and flaw in the Consumer's statement because the rant was impromptu, not well thought out. And if the soulless paid strict attention to what the Bitchy Rah said in its improvised and exhausting tirade, then the soulless can readily demonstrate the error in the Consumer's impression. This rule is as important as the first rule because often times a Fake Mouth will become a Bitchy Rah. Transformative beings these soul-suckers are. While observing both Rule 1 and Rule 2, the soulless must also keep a sharp eye out for Partner Rah.

Rule 3: <u>Always be on the lookout for a smoke screen</u>: Partner Rah can be both a cohort of some Abrasive Mouth, but Partner Rah can also be a Crafty Rah in actuality. These are sneaky crawling beings that are skilled and will leave only dead packaging behind if the soulless are not vigilant. The blitzkrieg assault is regularly deployed to distract a soulless from observing the actions of a 5Finger Rah. This is where the soulless must wait for 5Finger Rah to become either In-A-Hurry Rah or Looking At-The-Door Rah. It is at this point that I generally said something to the effect of have a good day sir to In-A-Hurry Rah. No way was I going to risk my soulless-self over some corporate profit margin.

The most robust smoke screens come from Banker Rahs. These are your money scammers; they are not interested in merchandise. Stupid people try to scam money, too, but they just suck at it so remember Rule 3.b: If it's fishy and high dollar, refuse it. The Consumer will express anger, but if a soulless allows a scam to work once then that Consumer will come back and pull it again on the same soulless individual. Let it suck on someone else's life force vein next time.

Rule 4: <u>Always watch an asshole walk away</u>. This is simple, when caterpillars are trying to pull the wool over a soulless' eyes, they will look back as they walk away, whether the scam worked or not. Honest Consumers, when upset and feel they've been wronged, will look defiantly ahead as they leave. But when that scheming, nefarious, obtuse, and Fat Mouth dunderhead walks away from rejection, its pride takes a hit on the way out. A retreating dog always looks back.

I know what you're thinking; how do I shut up and let the Consumer talk, always pay strict attention to what a Consumer says and does, and always be on the lookout for a smoke screen so that I know which Consumers to watch as they walk away. It's simple- shut-up and let the Consumer talk, always pay strict attention to what the Consumer says and does, and always be on the lookout for a smoke screen. How about an example?

I worked at Family Fun Bowling Center for an eternity or two. That place has been helping to create impromptu families since the sixties. Don't let *Fun* or *Family* fool you. This was unadulterated, grown folks territory. On this night, I was the shift supervisor, so I was the light to which the moths flocked. I wasn't exactly shocked to be informed, by a Consumer, that there was an issue in the bar. At times the bar was a thick and disgusting cloud of people and breath.

"Ey, man! Ey, man! Someone's swallowed glass in the bar, man. Your glass was broken."

This comes from a short, muscle-bound, square-shaped guy. He was twenty-something, wearing an extra-large t-shirt and denim pants that were wider than they were tall. And, of course, he wore a visor backward and upside down. So I knew immediately that this guy was attending the festivities with a partner because this brand of sex appeal doesn't fly solo.

At first, I thought that I misunderstood what Muscle Mouth said, so I joked.

"You have a shallow glass in the bar?"

"Yeah, man!" he replied, then he walked off.

I followed him to the bar anyway because it didn't really matter what he said. My job was simple. Solve problems. I said nothing, rule 1, and I was immediately suspicious because Glow-in-the-dark Bowling was happening. The bowling center and bar were dark, chaotic, crowded, and very annoying. Rule 2 - As we walked, I was focused on the square guy. He watched the bowling lanes and lights, not the glass double doors to the bar opposite his gaze. Muscle Mouth wasn't worried.

Muscle Mouth pushed through the dense crowd in the bar and straight to the lounge area kitty-corner from the entrance. Sitting on the pleather couch in the corner was a blond, almost pretty young girl sitting with a tall second Muscle Mouth. Standing on the opposite side of the coffee table in front of the couch, when we approached, was another young woman. A real Loud Mouth with a spare tire and big tin bracelets around both wrists. I had no choice but to start over. Rule 1: shut-up and let the Consumer talk.

Loud Mouth created the tension as she yelled on and on about how her friend, Glass Mouth, swallowed a piece of glass that was at the bottom of her beer glass. She used her fingers to indicate a piece of glass about three inches long, bracelets swaying soundlessly with each gesture. I could see from the broken glass on the table that a substantial portion of the glass was missing. I debated looking in the trash can, but not for too long.

Glass Mouth would have noticed such a large shard in her mouth immediately, like ice. Or I could ask Loud Mouth why she was watching her friend drink so astutely that she could describe the shard, but somehow could do nothing to stop Glass Mouth? Loud Mouth kept on like she was slick:

"You need to tell your fuckin' bartender to check the fuckin' ice. She swallowed a big ass piece of glass, dude. She might fuckin' die because of this. I swear, that fuckin' piece of glass was this goddamn big, and you need to tell the fuckin' bartender to change the fuckin' ice. She might die. She was fuckin' rude to me when I told her what she fuckin' did and shit. This is fuckin' bullshit! She was rude, and now she might die."

This was ten minutes of nonstop dialogue in that vein, with the occasional gasp for air. While Loud Mouth cycled redundantly, Muscle

58

Mouth 1 kept inching closer and closer to me as he chimed in.

"Exactly. Yeah. That was fuckin' uncalled for. Tell that bitch!"

Muscle Mouth 2 also chimed in, but less frequently:

"Yeah... Huh, uh huh... Pshshshshshshsh... Hah."

Glass Mouth just played the sad part of being on the verge of tears, sipping cautiously from her new glass of beer. The other three worked on the remainder of the pitcher vigilantly. I let this go on until Loud Mouth and the other three silently stared at me as though it was now my turn to speak. Loud Mouth shifted into neutral. Muscle Mouth 1 stared, red-faced, with his nonbeer hand pocketed and his visor now sideways and upside down. Muscle Mouth 2 and Glass Mouth just looked lost as I paused.

After having listened to everything that everyone in the group had to say, I responded.

"Well, this is serious. She can die. I'm gonna call an ambulance and get her to a doctor right away."

They refused, of course, and I insisted urgently several more times that we get her to a hospital. Each round of *your employee injured our friend* had less energy and volume until finally Loud Mouth thanked me for my concern and insured me that Glass Mouth would be okay. I urged my opinion that they should take her to an emergency room directly one last time, and then I resumed my other duties. You would think that to be the end of it, but no, these caterpillars want to eat.

I stood in the middle of the concourse watching the lanes and bowlers because people think they are invisible and they do stupid and dangerous shit. Things like run up the lane and fall on their ass, or stick their hands and head in the ball return. Those things really do happen.

As I watched and scanned for Destructive Rahs, a half-hour after our first encounter, the charismatic Muscle Mouth 1 approached me, his hat now on the other side of his head, right side up.

"Hey, man. Can we talk, man?" he said, tapping my shoulder. "Coo', that was fucked up. What happened backder. And man... I have a sociates's duhgree in law. So, man... thas fucked up. What happened. So, what-er you gonna do 'bout it, man?"

"Nothing."

"Nothing? Nothing at all?"

"I'll call an ambulance."

"Yore not even gonna comp us the beer, man? Thas fucked up! Izer everyone else I can talk to?"

"No."

"Well, whose yore boss?"

"The owner."

"Wares he?"

"I don't know."

"How can my loyer get a hoda him?"

"Wait here."

Muscle Mouth 1 stood and watched as I walked behind the desk and returned with the regular business card for the Family Fun Bowling Center - after answering the phone first. I handed it to him, he said "tanks, man. Shhhhit", and took the card before storming off. Once he was through the double doors, he looked back at me.

So, as I said before, it's as simple as following these four rules. If you can do that, then you, too, can be a caterpillar slayer.

Buy

If I were a zombie, I would be the zombie standing right next to the undead savage that got the kill, blood-spattered but slack-jawed. Which, I suppose, would also make me the zombie standing by the office blood warmer - that braindead idiot who moans on and on about *that one time I nearly caught the biggest fish ever*. All of that is precisely why I do not want to become a zombie.

Fresh out of the Marine Corps and in need of a job, I was fodder for the freelance shysters. All I could think to do was what every person on TV did when quick employment became necessary. I looked in the want ads in the local newspaper. Then I called the first ad I saw and arranged an interview with the person on the other end of the phone. That was the only phone call I made because I was of a mind to do each call and interview one after the other.

The ad called the business an "Advertisement Agency," which errs on the side of leniency in the definition of the chosen words. Some could even allude to foul odors when describing the accuracy of an ad such as the one I answered. Nonetheless, however, I was stupid and excited. Although I knew everything that I would ever need to know already, I also knew next to nothing about anything that I did need to know.

The next order of business was to buy some clothing that would be appropriate for a job interview because I was a man with a job interview. When I think about the outfit I assembled and purchased for this interview, I can see now that it was based mostly on how far from a uniform it was, while maintaining what was appropriate. The shirt was baggy and made of an odd choice of red, like the stain on the table cloth. The belt was for a person twice my size, and the pants were black and baggy. I tied it all together with my uniform dress shoes. And some necktie, too, of course.

I shot for fifteen minutes early, but rolled into the parking lot of the extra generic, bi-level set of leased office spaces thirty minutes early. With so much time on my hands, I did the most courteous thing I could think of to kill time. I smoked a bunch of cigarettes.

The time to appear in person came, and I went straight to the suite for Braindead Ads. I used no deodorizing sprays, no breath mints, just a ball of nose-blind nerves. Braindead Ads was not at all what I expected. I don't know what I expected exactly, but it did consist of more than three people and blank walls. Opposite the door, and in the corner to my right, was a desk with Phoney Brain behind it, on the phone at the time. I waited patiently because the braindead are generally slow.

To the left was a hallway that extended the visible space. On the side opposite my respective location was a long conference room. Opposite that were a couple of doors, offices likely. Directly ahead of me, behind Phoney, was a wide door. Three of me could walk through that door side-by-side.

"Hi, are you Jeff?"

She was either good at her job, or I was the only interviewee expected.

"Great, I'll let Matt know you're here. Just one moment." She uncradled the phone, pushed a button, then paused. "Jeff's here. You're welcome."

The wide door directly ahead of me opened within seconds and a slumping guy stepped out wearing a baggy, drab sort of banana-colored shirt. He had a buzz cut up top and huge feet under turd colored pants. With his hand out he opened the dialogue. That immediacy, I now know, was another red flag. This wasn't an ordinary "sell" that they had sniffed out by nose. No, this was a trap that they had lured my fresh meat into.

"Hi... buy... Wow, sorry. My name is Droneon Brain. You must be Jeff."

To this point, I still haven't said a single word. Being true to the Advertisers that they were, they insisted, emphatically, on doing most of the talking.

"Well, Matt Brain is on an important call with Corporate Headquarters."

"Buy him in, Droneon," came through the wide office doorway.

"Come on in, Jeff" Droneon said as he opened the door and motioned with his right claw for me to enter first.

"Jeff! Have a seat buddy. Thanks, Droneon." Matt was such a great guy, friendly and welcoming and it overflowed his five-foot-two body as he walked around the ten-person table that he used for a desk. "So, Jeff, Buddy, they tell me that you're a former Marine. Buy am too, buddy. I was motor pool, stationed at Fort Bragg. Three years and done, right?"

Motor pool is for company cars. In the Corps, it is known as Motor Transport but generally referred to as Motor-T. Fort Bragg is an

Army base, and Marine contracts were four or five years at that time, but not three.

"That's why I want to help you out, Jeff. I have a great opportunity for you, Buddy, because what we do here is make competitive management material. How do we do that? Let me tell you."

Matt's natural pauses were present through inflection only. There was no actual break in speech. I didn't see him take a single breath.

"What we do here, is we train people to be aggressive about their success. That's right, we are the first rung on that ladder, and I wanna put you on the road to being a rich man, Jeff. Buddy."

Matt's whole pitch kept on and on. He went into his experience in marketing, how he came to it. He spoke of the man who mentored him into the business like he had a rock star's prostate.

"Last year, I cleared a hundred grand. You don't believe me, right? I'll take you to my car in the parking lot to see my car. I spend the day playing golf, man. I don't work anymore. My wife? Gorgeous trophy wife. She doesn't love me, but I buy her diamonds. I buy her jewelry. I buy her expensive trips to the Bahamas... Buy, buy, BUY... Oh, sorry. I'm getting a little, throat thing, or something. Buy hey, Jeff... Buddy! We'll buy you lunch, and all you gotta do is give me a chance to change your life. What'dya say? Free lunch, a chance at the good life? How *could* you say no?"

Matt never actually explained what the company did as far as I could figure. He did, however, ask me for a second interview the next day. When I agreed, he called Droneon back in.

"This guy's my guy, Buddy. He's gonna show you the ropes. This guy, Jeff, he was the best braindead associate I had. He's gonna teach you how to become a full manager like me. When they gave me my own office, and they asked who I wanted as my number two, I said this buy right here. He's not as good as me, but he's good. Albuy Jeff, Drone's gonna take it from here. Thanks for coming. Remember Jeff, if nothing else, you get a free lunch."

Droneon escorted me three steps from the wide door, which then closed.

"Awesome, Jeff. Looks like Matt like's you. So tomorrow's a big day. See you buy here at nine, I wanna get an early start. See you tomorrow. Buy, buy, now."

I walked across the broad, nondescript, reception room and they watched me walk. I went home excited that I had a follow-up interview but confused over what I was interviewing for. Over dinner at a barbeque restaurant that night, I couldn't actually explain what the company did. The napkin was about the same color as my dress shirt when I was done.

I slept in a bit, got out on the right side of the bed, and then prepared myself for my 9:00 AM sequel with Braindead Ads. I got there about thirty minutes early, again, smoked a bunch of cigarettes in the car, again, neglected to spray or mint, again, and went back into the nondescript waiting room, again. This time Phoney wasn't alone in the room, however. Three ladies younger than myself were also in the waiting room, waiting.

Hellos went in rounds like a roulette ball, but *hi,... Jeff* was all I contributed to the conversation between those girls in the waiting room. I don't think that I went much deeper than that for the duration of the affair, but neither did they. We were eventually herded, by Droneon, into the conference room I mentioned before.

"Buy everybody! This way, please. Matt wanted to be here, buy he had urgent family matters, so it's gonna be just us today. Please, have a seat everybody."

Droneon flipped open his flip board with legs. He swung it a bit vigorously, and it landed hard, rocking the tripod stand a bit.

"Sorry! Got away from me. Didn't get enough buy this morning."

69

The flip chart guided Droneon through a lecture on the workings of a pyramid scheme. Matt, at the top of the office, made the most money because Corporate Headquarters rewarded him with this office for his hard work. Matt was allowed an unlimited number of people under him. Droneon was an Assistant Manager. He was allowed to have twenty people under him, working for him.

"So I'm looking for people like you to be my Assistant Training Managers. You see when you get to where I'm at, you can have your Assistant Training Managers do all the work while you stay at home buying video games. Or, you stay in the office and find more Assistant Training Managers. What does an Assistant Training Manager do? You train Recruit Managers. People like yourselves. As Assistant Training Managers, you can buy as many as thirty people under you, workin' hard to make you money."

The girls were all very impressed by the possibilities of such a setup once Droneon stopped reciting words at us. Next came the engine for all of these piles of money - he was going to reveal the secret to all this success.

"We advertise for other companies buy... buy selling promotional packages that they buy..., buy... send to us."

70

The package that was being pitched at the time was a prepaid weekend deal to Las Vegas. I don't remember the details, but they were the same crap as all of those rouses. The incentive for us, the braindead recruits, is that we, starting that moment, were eligible to receive a one dollar commission on every sale of that promo pack. Should we become Assistant Training Managers, we were to earn five dollars per sale of their promos as well as five dollars for the sale of every promo from the Recruit Managers under us. Droneon was an Assistant Manager, so he received a ten dollar commission for every promo, but those were not the big bucks by any stretch.

"Matt. He's a Manager. He gets thirty bucks for his buys, thirty bucks for mine, and thirty bucks for yours. That man buy..., buy... cleared a hundred and fifty buy..., buy... fifty... buy..., buy... a hundred and fifty thousand last year."

And just how, one could ask, does one become an Assistant Training Manager? We had to first pass the field portion of the interview, and finally, we had to pass a test back at Braindead Ads, afterward. From there it was into the big time. I wasn't thrilled by the revelation, but I just went along with it. But it smelled foolish.

"So, it'd be better if we all went in the same buy. Anyone have a car that's big enough? Ladies?"

"I was dropt off, so..."

"No, uh uhn."

"What time is it?"

"Jeff, what do you drive?"

"A four-door."

"You okay with driving, Jeff? My car doesn't have a backseat."

"Sure, I guess."

"Great. Let's hit the buy..., buy... bricks, beople."

Myself, the faded banana, and the Three Amigas, dressed like they're going to a night club, piled into my car. Suzy and I drove at that time a white 1998 Volks Wagon Jetta, not small but not big either. A healthy layer of dust caked the paint, and the inside of the car was a bit messy. It must have smelled like an atomic ashtray inside, but hey, they didn't say anything about me driving anyone around. I was in the driver's seat, obviously, Droneon rode shotgun, and the Three Amigas compressed themselves into the back seat.

The first stop we made was to a liquor store so that Droneon could get some breath mints. The Three Amigas reapplied such things as makeup and cleavage as they chattered in their sardine can.

"Whose done this be four? I did latts weekend."

"Yeah, uh huh."

"Does anyone have any gum?"

"You too? With Gary?"

"No, uh uhn."

"Never mind, I have some gum. Wait no. Who has gum?"

"This's a graaate oppertunaty. You don't all'weez get oppertutaties like this."

"Yeah, uh huh."

I just watched Droneon in the liquor store. He was pitching the Vegas weekend promo to the cashier. I don't think the kid could gamble, but Droneon didn't seem to care.

"What 'bout yew, Jeff? You done this all-ready?"

"Nah. This is the first time for me."

"I did it latts weekend, with Gary. He's cool."

"Yeah, uh huh."

"Wait, you did this already, Jeff?"

This was the nature of the conversation until Droneon came back. He carried with him the same number of promo packs that he entered the store with. He was still upbeat, though.

"So yeah, buys. I tried to get a sell with the cashier in there. I didn't get the sell, buy that brings me to your first and most important lesson, buy... Every 'no' brings you closer to your next 'yes.' Matt makes more than a hundred seventy buy dollars a year because he gets as many 'no's' as possible."

"Oh my god, that'so deep. It's like, obvious but, but still true. I never thought 'bout it like that."

"Yea, uh huh, right?"

"So, he said yes in there?"

"Well, there's a spot that I drove buy the other day that looked good. I always wanted, buy... buy... to give it a try. I'll direct you where to buy, Jeff. Blet's hit the road."

I parked the car for the first leg of the day. The banana, the red stain, and the Three Amigas began our fieldwork right out of the car. The first pitch came quick, and I didn't see it start. I turned, and suddenly Droneon was in some guy's face.

"Buy... Buy... Buy... Buy... Buy..."

The walker-by was taken by surprise, but he was able to beat Droneon back eventually. Undeterred, Droneon went from one person to the next, droning on and on about that Vegas promo. Some of the crowd avoided eye contact and walked by him, fast. Others barked their disinterest. The weak, however, were cornered and forced to fight their way out of Droneon's grasp.

Finally, a security guard came to the public's rescue.

"Damn braindead pests. Get outta here, pal."

"Buy... Buy... Buy..."

We left, but Droneon had a nose for crowds, and he was hungry. On foot and en route to a nest, he explained to us.

"You see that buy... buy... You see that back there? That was a lot of no's, so I'm real close to buy... next yes. That's how Matt came to buy a full manager. He makes more than two hundred, buy... buy... and fifty thousand a year. Not buy, huh? You buys feel free to hang buy and watch if you need, buy jump in when you're ready. Buy..."

We hit strip malls, gas stations, bus stops, and even a roaming dog groomer. Droneon deflected dozens of no's at a time, but he fought eagerly for that next yes. Lunchtime came, and it was time for me to receive payment for my inclusion in the day's activities. In the car, I drove around looking for a place to eat because Droneon didn't know the area. From the horizon rose a Carl's Jr.

This Carl's looked like it had been a truck stop at one time. Right off of an eight-lane street, the parking lot was huge. The lot could accommodate the crowd in a small stadium. The line was lunch long, but I was hungry, and lunch was looking to be the highlight of the day. In the crowd that was being passed off as a line, I asked Droneon if he wanted to place the order while the rest of us found a table. The puzzled look on his face answered my question.

"Ahh, well..."

"Matt said that lunch was on you guys."

"Ahh, yeah. It is. I'll buy I guess."

Lunch was uneventful. Afterward, we found the mother-load of generic office spaces. Droneon began pitching people walking around, and the girls even tried to get some sells.

"Don't you wanna buy this. Buy this pleez. Buy. I want you to buy."

"Yeah, uh huh, buy. Buy, right? Yeah, uh huh, buy. Buy buy."

"What is this? What do I do with it? How do you do this? Wait, who's Gary?"

I just watched. Nearly every door that Droneon walked through had a sign that explicitly stated, "NO SOLICITING." The Three Amigas milled around, taking random, poorly executed attempts on pedestrians. I was bored, and I also grew to detest the idea of doing that. Finally, the moment came as we walked back to the car for the final time. Droneon came in for the sell.

"So Jeff, buddy. What'da ya think? Can you do this? Are you ready for the test? Do you want the opportunity to make more than three hundred thousand a year, like Matt?"

"Droneon? Is there a base salary for this job?"

"No. Just commission."

That should have been my first question to those people.

I knew that I should have waited, but I told Droneon, "Sorry man, but this just isn't for me."

That made for an awkward drive back to Braindead Ads, but I just didn't want to be a zombie.

They worked for John's Bug Killers

Bowling, as a physical sport, has the uncanny ability to make even the most athletic and the most graceful people look ridiculous. I have seen a high school basketball team come in and look like they started learning how to walk right there on the approaches. It's disgusting, with body parts jutting out here, crumpling up there but in the wrong places, and horrible sounds bursting from both ends. It can get ugly on the boards of the approach.

I want you to imagine someone in a leg cast limping, or throwing a discus, or even tossing a stick in the wind. Those are some of the varied ways that drunks look when they're trying to bowl. They think that they are smooth and slick like the bowlers on TV or the internet, but they can't even get the ball onto their own lane and stay on their feet in the same shot.

The Family Fun Bowling Center had nine o'clock specials, a time when nobody wanted to bowl, but they want to drink a lot because they have kids. Cheap bowling simply provided cheap entertainment and babysitters for the drunks in need of a watering hole. The cheaper it was to bowl, the more demanding the customers and their beady-eyed, buck-toothed, snot-smeared, huge mess-making, and demanding kids. Two kids and two pitchers of soda translates to a black, sticky floor and approach for hundreds of square feet. The parents just walked in it.

Sunday night wasn't the cheapest night, but it was still demanding, because, on a date, greasy foods, drinks, and dirty balls are all part of the romance. Sometimes those Sunday nights were rainy and extra drunk. Some Sunday nights, however, were unique because, to my displeasure, the general public had the following Monday morning off. But some Sunday nights, horrible Sunday nights, the unhappy family types had the next morning off, and the rain was flooding the snack bar with water. I don't usually talk about those Sundays.

So there I was, Sunday night before Spring Break begins, the snack bar is bitching about all the water coming through the ceiling, and I've been pondering profound, introspective questions like, *do I hate my job or do I hate my life?* So in truth, it was just the start to another week of servicing the general public's boredom. And their grubby, poorly behaved kids.

As the porter and desk guy moved to and fro, cleaning up after the finishing league that bowled Sunday evenings, I looked at the ugly, smelly, and rain-soaked swarm of cheap bowlers that called themselves a line. With larvae in hand, they waited eagerly to get their hands on food and drink and balls. The line flooded from one end of the center to the other and in line stood many, many children and teenagers. Shit!

These crowds will only remain a rustled group until the flood gates are opened, so crowd control is a must as one group pushes into the current group's space. It's like bumper dominoes. The best crowd control is consistency from one shift to another. When these mindless brainiacs know what to expect, they behave a little better.

Check-in, as the jargon went, was one of the singularly most redundant and frustrating things I've ever done. Have you ever wondered how many people know their shoe size? Well, the answer is less than those who do. The worst, however, and call me weird, but I have this thing about answering a question with a question, I despise it. For example:

Desk Employee: "What size shoes do you need?"

Human: "Uhm... Do they run big or small?"

Desk Employee: "They're pretty true to size."

Human: "Okay, uhm... Hey Friend, what size do you wear?"

Friend: "What size what?"

Human: "Oh my god, you're so stupid. He ha he ha. What size shoe size. He ha he ha he ha."

Friend: "oh, ha he ha he ha he. I think like a eight or nine."

Human: "God, you are no help, he ha he ha."

Desk Employee: "What size would you like to try?"

Human: "Uhm,... give me a eight or nine."

Now do that for every group looking to bowl for up to twenty-four individual groups. But that's just shoes. Now we must gather some more vital information.

Employee: "How many people are in your group?"

Human: "How much does it cost to bowl?"

Employee: "Blah, blah, blah per person. How many are in your group?"

Human: "Do we have to pay all together, or can we pay separately?"

Employee: "Yes"

Silence.

Human: "So, can... do we pay together, or... "

Employee: "You can all pay separately. How many are in your group?"

Human: "Do you guys take cards?"

Employee: "We do. How many are bowling?"

Human: "Oh, hey guys... who's bowling?"

This would happen for all twenty-four lanes. I'll spare you the horror of collecting fifteen or twenty separate payments from scrambling teens who forgot that there is no such thing as a free lunch. But that is how an average check-in would go.

On this Sunday night, people were wading through the snack bar and people didn't have to get up and take their dirty kids to school, so we had far more groups of humans looking to bowl then we had lanes for them to bowl on. We hit capacity about halfway through the line and filled out a waiting list with another fifteen groups.

Pete and Repeat came up to the desk from the back of the line. Pete looks around at the chaos that about 120 people were inflicting on my shift and he drank beer from a glass he held like a can. Repeat just stood and looked at me with a glass in one hand and a pitcher in the other. The look on his face suggested that he was waiting to see if his fart stinks.

"Is there any way you could get us a lane?" Pete finally asks.

"Yeah, anyway at all, man?" Repeat repeats.

I would get this question a lot, and I don't know if people thought we had a VIP room, or maybe a rollout set of overflow lanes, but the answer seemed to bewilder Pete and Repeat.

"Nope, but I can put you on the waiting list."

"Is it long, man?"

"Yeah, is it long?"

"Five billion people ahead of you," I replied

Pete looked out at the lanes, then at Repeat, then at the list, then back at the lanes.

"It's just that, we came here with our families, bro', and the kids wanna bowl."

"Yeah man, they wanna bowl, bro'."

"We didn't know it wuz gonna be so busy. We work for John's Bug Killers."

"Yeah, for John's Bug Killers, dude."

John, of John's Bug Killers, was a regular league bowler and he advertised his business on the electronic scoreboards, so I knew the reference, and I knew John. Not well, but I knew when to find him at the bowling center.

"I wish I could help you guys, but they're all taken. But I'll put you on the list. Most people get bored after ten or fifteen minutes and leave, so it's not as bad as it looks."

"Thanks, man."

"Yeah, thanks, man."

I went back to my job, which on a night like that night consisted mostly of me, the desk guy, and the porter doing our best to keep those people from burning the place down. I made a couple of calls over the speakers reminding bowlers about things like only one person being allowed to bowl at a time. Someone asked me if I could turn the Glow-In-the-Dark Bowl lights on for just their lanes and as soon as I said no, it's not possible, I heard a CRACK as a bowling ball bounced off of a rake. The rake is the arm that sweeps the pins away once they've been lifted.

As always, I went to the lane and retrieved the ball as it rolled backwards toward the bowlers. I did this even when the ball wouldn't have stopped somewhere midway because I wanted to ensure that the people who are busting up the machines know that I know what they did, you know?

When I got back to the desk, not ten minutes after our first conversation, Pete and Repeat came back up.

"How's it lookin'? You got anything yet?"

"Yeah, you got anything yet, man. How's it lookin'?"

"Nothing yet."

"Cuz you know, we work for John's Bug Killers and John bowls here."

"Yeah, you know. He bowls here."

"If anything opens up for you, I'll let you guys know," I uttered habitually.

"It's just that, he brings business here."

"That's right. He brings...

"We do our company conferences in the bar every year."

"Every year, for like the last two..."

"Yeah man, the last two years now."

We wound circles like that for a couple of minutes, and we danced like that three more times before I finally got a set of lanes back that I could put them on. They kept throwing John's Bug Killers around like John was a co-owner of Family Fun Bowling Center. I remained patient because drunks only become more annoying in a confrontation. They love to tell people to listen.

"Alright guys, how many in the group?"

"Ahh... well, uhhhhh." Repeat ponders before Pete makes it to the desk.

"Hey, what's up, dude? Finally, huh?"

"How many in your group?"

"Well, hey uhh..." he looks at Repeat. "Hey dude, is Repeated bowling?"

"I don't know, bro. Did she say she was gonna bowl?"

"Is my wife bowling, hey pumkin', ask Mom if they're bowling. Hang on, Dude."

Pumpkin came back and said no. After a round of questions and answers passed through various kids, Pete and Repeat decided that just the kids were gonna bowl, so I put all thirty or forty of them on two lanes, tried seven or eight different pairs of shoes for each kid, and then I was done. John's Bug Killers were out of my hair. Or so I thought.

About fifteen minutes later, as I walked along the concourse putting out fires, I heard a loud CRACK. I looked back, and a ball was speeding back toward Pete on lane 3. While I was walking toward his lane, he threw apologies my way, and another CRACK came as Repeat did the same thing on lane 4.

"Don't hit the rake, guys."
"Sorry, bro."
"Yeah, bro.
"Sorry, man."
"Sorry."
"Look at the pins before you shoot."
"Yeah."
"Yeah."
"Sorry."
"Sorry."

I kept it real friendly because these guys were in front of a good ten or twelve of their kids, even though they weren't supposed to be bowling and they weren't wearing shoes. I told them they

87

needed to come to the desk and get bowling shoes if they wanted to bowl.

"What size shoes do you need guys?"

"Do they run big or small?"

"Ten" Repeat said.

"Pretty true to size."

"Ah, probably like uh…"

"Look in your shoe, dude." Repeat for the win, again. "That's what my mom always said." Then he held his left shoe out for me to take.

"No, thanks, you can keep your shoes, man. Just bring ours back up to the desk, please."

I went back to my job drunksitting and babysitting. I had kids of any age running freely on any horizontal surface including the seat backs and lanes. I had adults blowing ass all over a stall in each the Men's and Women's rooms. I would have felt bad for the porter, but I did my time on the shit-end of that stick. Human feces in the open air is a vile substance.

Some kid about eighteen or so ran desperately to the restroom, hand over mouth. But, no. Chunks and bile spewed from this kid like a geyser, and he sprayed it all over the carpet right in front of the desk, which was right where my nose spent the majority of any given night.

As I was helping the porter with Geyser Mouth's mess, I heard another CRACK. I stood and spun around to see a ball shooting back at

Pete on lane 3. I stormed down the stairs to lanes 3 and 4, retrieved the ball, and then placed it on the ball return. I stared at Pete both times I passed him in the bowler's waiting area. I wanted to yell whatever flew from my teeth at him and kick him out. However, his young daughter stood near him, and I didn't want to tear into him in front of his kid, so I just fumed and stared.

By midnight I was ready to kick everybody out and get out of the building myself, but the place was a wreck. I made the ten-minute announcement that the lanes would be shutting off, not that it ever did any good. Then I politely announce that people needed to quit hurling balls up their lanes because the machines are going to shut down immediately. Again, it did no good.

I pushed the button on the computer screen, and the lanes all powered down. Of course, a couple dozen or so balls were thrown anyway. People began to bring their disgusting shoes up to us. Two minutes after the last bowling ball was thrown, I was spraying disinfectant into the shoes, and I heard a CRACK.

Pete rolled a ball at the rake again. Repeat was elsewhere, and one of Pete's daughters was still with him. I was definitely angry by that point, but again I seethed as I stared at him going by the first time because his daughter was right there. I grabbed the ball from the gutter and kept it as I

89

seethed going by the second time. Only this time, as I walked away, Pete opened his mouth.

"Hey, you don't unnerstand. That wassen my fault, dude. I work for John's Bug Killers. Lissin'a me dude! I werk fer John's and I would'en... "

I do not remember exactly what I said, but I was holding a bowling ball, and I remember a look of shock on his face as he backed up. I said something to the effect of

"You new goddamn fucking well what you were doing, so don't give me that horse shit."

I also tend to use a lot of hand gestures when I talk. After I walked up the steps to the concourse, Pete followed me with more of the same as I took the bowling ball back to the ball room. It was actually labeled Ball Room with neon lights.

"Hey man. Lissin'a me, man. Don't walk away frume, dude."

As I walked back to the desk, toward Pete, he approached me, and Repeat was back in the game. They both stepped in front of me, and our toes were all nearly touching. I held where my feet landed and moved my gaze from one to the other as they both talked over each other.

"Hey, that, that shit, that's whore's shit. That wassen my fault, dude. I werek at John's Bug Killerrrs. He brings buzness here, man. Ev'ry year, man. He spends money in this building, dude and youj'st walk away frume? That's Bull SHHHit. I spent my muney in'er too, man. And I work fur John's Bug Killers, dude. Bullshit."

"It is bull's shit... yore machines su, chines suck... a long time now... fuckin' loyal cussumer all the times he's here man. Bull's shits and we work for John... fuckin' dog shit, bro."

These guys just kept on like that, so I interrupted them.

"Okay, well tell me guys, what is your boss gonna think when my boss calls him and tells him all about how two of his employees behaved, busting up his expensive equipment while they repeatedly threw the name of his company around?"

Each of their eyes moved away from me as they processed my statement. Then they turned around and walked straight for the front doors because they worked for John's Bug Killers.

That was just the going rate for a sunflower seed

I went through probably six or seven rodents growing up. We would get about a year from mice and two from hamsters. My first hamster was a biter, and I took care of him, but when he died a year later, I wasn't sad. I learned that the trick to picking a rodent from the many potential biters in those tanks was to get the youngest one. They didn't allow kids to handle their animals for some reason, so you had to watch them react to the employee's hand. Some biters run, and some show their teeth, but sometimes they bite first. When rodents are handled daily at a young age, however, they are very docile and will even jump into your hand.

The rodent that started it all off, however, was a mouse we named Goldie. I got Goldie from a friend at school, and this mouse was, gram for gram, the fattest rodent I ever had. After a couple of weeks at home, this rodent wouldn't come out of her enclosure except to eat and drink. No exercise wheel action at all. This was the laziest pet, I thought, and I was not wrong.

One day I looked in the cage and Goldie was going in and out of the enclosure and pushing something around inside it. A closer inspection revealed a bunch of pinkies in her home. That was pretty cool for a little while, but it wasn't long before those little bastards were climbing through the bars and running around all night. They couldn't get off the tall cabinet that the cage was on, but it was still aggravating to have to catch them every morning. But that meant that they were ready to leave Goldie and become someone else's stinky mess.

I somehow found people to take five mice, and we kept one for Jared, my younger brother. I kept Goldie's lazy ass, of course. Snooper, a scrawny, black escape artist with extra-large testicles, was Jared's mouse. That mouse refused to accept his situation, but he had been handled since Goldie was done with him, so when we caught him he didn't bite. He would crap right into your hand, though.

For the first few months of Snooper's life, he could just squeeze through the bars. That mouse was, gram for gram, the strongest rodent I've ever seen. We tried everything and anything we could think of to keep him from climbing the bars, like duck tape liners around the bars, but he only had one purpose in life. Freedom.

Then, for a few months, Jared just forgot to close the gate to his cage quite often. He claimed that Snooper could push the cage door open. For the remainder of Snooper's life, my youngest brother Cory, a toddler at the time, just thought it was funny to open the cage and let Snooper out. Snooper spoke toddler, I guess. But it could have been that we didn't, for some reason, move the cage up and out of my diapered brother's reach.

That mouse knew our house better than we did. At first, he would just watch us from the corner of a furniture piece or an open door. But eventually, he would stand in the middle of the kitchen floor and wait for someone to run in for the snag. Then he broke the sound barrier on his way to safety.

He would run across the room along the baseboards in the living room while everyone was watching TV. That little bastard taunted us, but like I said, if you could catch him, he was a great pet. Sometimes he even ate a sunflower seed for me while he crapped in my hand.

The longer Snooper was out of his cage, the bolder he became and the tougher catching him became. We used everything from sunflower seeds, to cereal, to peanut butter to bait him.

Snooper was always shy about the bait the first few days, so we had to place food near one of his runs. He would sit in a cubby between the TV stand and the wall, safe from hands, and stare at the seed or whatever. At times I sat or laid and stared at him in there, and he just sat on his balls and stared back.

After about a week Snooper would run and grab. It was dangerous, but he was calculating. After two weeks he was just standing in the middle of the floor and laughing. He wasn't worried anymore. Once Snooper was out for more than four weeks, and we saw a level of boldness that can only be described as cocky. He didn't get out by negligence or jest on that adventure, however.

January 17, Martin Luther King Jr. Day, 4:30 am, I awoke in a panic and I tried to get out of bed, but couldn't. I pushed with my legs and twisted around, but I just couldn't get my bearings. I struggled as hard as I could but made no progress. Suddenly I fell calm, and I stopped struggling and walked out of my room.

Standing in the doorway from my room to the kitchen, in candlelight, I could see all of the heavy furniture and appliances moved about a foot from the wall. Dishes were strewn and broken everywhere, and in my room, the furniture covered the floor completely. At magnitude 6.7, the '94 Northridge earthquake took a devastating toll on L.A. County and its outlying areas.

We had to evacuate our house due to our proximity to a gas station. As we drove up Laurel Canyon Boulevard, a side street that we passed was on fire. The cars were burning, the palm trees were burning, and flames danced from a storm drain several feet high. This quake buckled streets, brought down steel and concrete overpasses, and collapsed the top two stories of the Northridge Mall into the third subfloor. It also caused the demolition of many other structures.

When we returned home and lifted the heavy cabinets, we found Snooper's cage open but no sign of Snooper. Goldie's cage was open and right side up. Goldie was inside with her food bowl, still full, and her water bottle still functional. The house wasn't back together for more than a few hours before Snooper started showing up. He would stare at us from the corners and run out from under the couch. That mouse ran circles around us before we finally caught him. We saw levels of risk never even heard of with that mouse. He also ran through my hand at one point and grabbed a sunflower seed before I could get a hold of him. In the seed's place was a little black, hotdog-shaped turd.

Made in the USA
Monee, IL
12 April 2021